Michelle Obama
HEALTH ADVOCATE

BY CLARA MacCARALD

Published by The Child's World®
1980 Lookout Drive • Mankato, MN 56003-1705
800-599-READ • www.childsworld.com

Photographs ©: Star Shooter/MediaPunch/Ipx/AP Images, cover, 1; Everett Collection/
Shutterstock Images, 5; Douliery Olivier/Sipa USA/AP Images, 6; Patsy Lynch/Rex
Features/AP Images, 9; Rex Features/AP Images, 10; Jay LaPrete/AP Images, 13; Chip
Somodevilla/Sipa USA/AP Images, 14; Almagro/Sipa USA/AP Images, 17; Anthony
Behar/Sipa USA/AP Images, 18

ISBN 9781503824027
LCCN 2017944744

Printed in the United States of America
PA02362

ABOUT THE AUTHOR

Clara MacCarald is a freelance writer with a master's degree in biology. She
lives with her family in an off-grid house nestled in the forests of central
New York. When not parenting her daughter, she spends her time writing
nonfiction books for kids.

TABLE OF
CONTENTS

FAST FACTS

Full Name

- Michelle LaVaughn Robinson Obama

Birthdate

- January 17, 1964, in Chicago, Illinois

Husband

- President Barack Hussein Obama

Children

- Malia and Sasha Obama

Years in White House

- 2009–2017

Accomplishments

- Began Let's Move!, an **initiative** that fought childhood **obesity**.
- Helped pass the Healthy, Hunger-Free Kids Act to improve the **nutrition** of school lunches.
- Started Joining Forces to help **veterans** find jobs and opportunities.

Chapter 1

A GROUNDBREAKING FIRST LADY

In March 2009, Michelle Obama, the new First Lady of the United States, stepped outside into the cool air. She walked across the South Lawn of the White House to join a group of giggling fifth graders. They rolled up their sleeves and eyed the tools that surrounded them. They were ready to start an **organic** garden. Michelle was dressed in a belted sweater and black boots. Despite her nice clothes, the First Lady was excited to get to work. Cameras clicked as she and the kids took up shovels and pitchforks to dig up the ground.

The work went slowly, but Michelle didn't lose her enthusiasm. "Hey, all of you," she called to reporters.

◀ A portion of the food grown in Michelle Obama's organic garden was donated to homeless shelters.

"Put down your cameras and pick up a shovel."[1] Afterward, they all had a snack of cider, apples, and shovel-shaped cookies. "Let's hear it for vegetables," Michelle said. Some kids cheered. "Did I hear a boo?" she joked.[2]

Throughout her eight years as First Lady, Michelle kept both her sense of style and her sense of humor. And she kept a focus on kids. Growing up in Chicago, Illinois, Michelle was close with her parents and brother. They often played games and took trips together.

Michelle also worked hard at school, staying up late to finish homework. With that hard work came opportunities. She attended Harvard Law School. She met Barack Obama in 1989 when they both worked at the same law office. Barack would stay late and sit on her desk to chat with her. They married in 1992 and had two daughters, Malia and Sasha.

In 2008, after a historic campaign, the nation chose Barack as its 44th president. On January 20, 2009, Michelle and Barack drove up to the White House.

▲ Michelle helped harvest vegetables
grown in the garden.

They were in a **limousine**. Michelle was happy for her
husband but nervous about how their life would change.
When they stepped outside into the freezing winter air,
they were greeted by a huge crowd that cheered for the
first black president and First Lady.

Chapter 2

MEDIA MOMENTS

Applause greeted Michelle as she walked onto the brightly lit stage. She looked out into the crowd of excited faces. Ellen DeGeneres, the talk show host, walked forward and wrapped her in a hug before they settled down into red armchairs. Michelle was ready to tell viewers about Let's Move!, an initiative she started to help fight obesity through healthy eating and movement.

Michelle enjoyed talking about exercising almost as much as she loved doing it. "How many push-ups can you do?" Ellen asked.[3] The audience laughed. "I can do some," Michelle replied.[4] Ellen challenged her to a contest, and Michelle was happy to accept.

◀ Michelle danced with Ellen DeGeneres to promote Let's Move!

> "Today I wake up every morning in a house that was built by slaves. And I watch my daughters, two beautiful, intelligent, black young women playing with their dogs on the White House lawn. And because of Hillary Clinton, my daughters and all our sons and daughters now take for granted that a woman can be president of the United States."[14]
>
> —Michelle Obama, campaigning for Hillary Clinton in 2016

The audience cheered as both women set their jackets aside and took to the floor for a push-up contest.

Michelle used TV appearances and the Internet to spread the word about Let's Move! She strove to get people excited about being healthy.

In 2014, Michelle entered the crowded set of Sesame Street. She loved appearing on the children's show. She sat at a table covered by a checkered tablecloth. A healthy breakfast was set in front of Michelle just as

▲ Michelle and Jill Biden, the wife of Vice President Joe Biden, partnered with Sesame Street to honor National Guard members.

the Muppet character Grover appeared. Underneath his furry exterior was a puppet master.

This puppet master controlled Grover's actions. "Wait a minute," Grover said in an excited voice. "Are you First Lady Mrs. Michelle Obama?"[6]

She replied, "I am, Grover. Hi, how are you?"[7] After Michelle explained the importance of a healthy breakfast to Grover and the audience, Grover ate the First Lady's breakfast. With a sad face, but laughing eyes, Michelle held up an empty bowl to the camera.

Chapter 3

GIRLS JUST WANT TO SUCCEED

The South Lawn of the White House was unrecognizable in June 2015. It was covered by a flock of white tents. Michelle joined a group of 50 Girl Scouts, who were delighted to have been invited to the first South Lawn campout ever. Wearing a white, sleeveless top, Michelle welcomed them to the White House with a smile. She pointed to stations where the campers could gain Girl Scout badges by performing activities. "I don't know if I can officially earn a badge," she said, "but I wanna try!"[8]

Michelle set up a tent and tied ropes with the girls. Later, her husband joined them as they sat on hay bales.

◀ Girl Scouts sang with Michelle and Barack during the White House campout.

Before them was a mock campfire made of lanterns. The girls sang, their voices ringing out into the quiet night. Finally, the couple headed back to the White House. "Keep it down tonight," Michelle said with a grin. "Just kidding. Have fun!"[9]

Michelle supported many other opportunities for kids. In June 2016, Michelle, her mother, and her daughters toured Liberia, a country in West Africa. They were supporting Let Girls Learn, an **international** initiative for female education. Girls in countries such as Liberia don't always have educational opportunities. Michelle visited a camp that taught young girls to be leaders. "I want you to keep fighting and stay in school," she told them.[10]

Michelle gave speeches to educate people on the ▶
Let Girls Learn initiative.

Chapter 4

LOOKING TO THE FUTURE

In June 2016, under a gray New York City sky, Michelle took the stage in front of a sea of students in black robes. More than 3,800 seniors were graduating that day from City College. The students burst into thunderous applause as they laid eyes on their First Lady. Michelle was moved by their affection. "This is a big day for me too," she said. "See, this is my very last **commencement** address as First Lady of the United States."[11]

"Just look at who you are," she told them. The students came from more than 150 different countries. "You speak more than 100 different languages."[12] Michelle was proud of what they had accomplished.

◄ Michelle gave 23 graduation speeches during her time as First Lady.

> "Today I wake up every morning in a house that was built by slaves. And I watch my daughters, two beautiful, intelligent, black young women playing with their dogs on the White House lawn. And because of Hillary Clinton, my daughters and all our sons and daughters now take for granted that a woman can be president of the United States."[14]
>
> —*Michelle Obama, campaigning for Hillary Clinton in 2016*

"So I want you all to go out there," she said. "Be great."[13]

In 2016, Michelle also spoke in support of Hillary Clinton's campaign for president. When Barack's presidency ended on January 20, 2017, the Obamas did not leave town. They stayed in Washington, DC, to let their younger daughter, Sasha, finish high school.

In March 2017, a group of 14 Washington, DC, high school students sat in a circle to wait for a special guest. They were expecting a school official.

Instead, Michelle walked in. She had come to hear about their struggles and goals. The students burst into tears and hugged her. Michelle accepted their hugs with a smile. She was grateful that she could continue to make a difference in people's lives even though her time as First Lady had ended.

THINK ABOUT IT

- The president is sometimes called the commander in chief. Michelle has called herself the mom in chief. Do you think this title fits her?
- Michelle won the hearts of many as First Lady. What do you think people liked about her?
- Michelle did many different things while her husband was the president. What do you think people will remember most about her?

GLOSSARY

commencement (kuh-MENS-ment): Commencement is an event held when students graduate. Michelle gave a commencement speech to graduating students.

initiative (in-ISH-uh-tiv): An initiative is a project that works toward a specific goal. Michelle began an initiative to make children healthier.

international (in-tur-NASH-uh-nuhl): Something that is international has to do with more than one country. Michelle supported an international plan that teaches young girls to be leaders.

limousine (lim-uh-ZEEN): A limousine is a long luxury car. The Obamas rode a limousine to their new home, the White House.

nutrition (noo-TRISH-uhn): Nutrition is the process of getting the food necessary for health and growth. Michelle strove to help kids receive good nutrition.

obesity (oh-BEE-si-tee): Obesity is the state of being very overweight. Michelle organized a program called Let's Move! to fight childhood obesity.

organic (or-GAN-ik): Organic plants are produced without artificial fertilizers or chemicals. Michelle created an organic garden at the White House.

veterans (VET-ur-uhns): Veterans are people who have been in the military. Michelle helped veterans find jobs.

SOURCE NOTES

1. Marian Burros. "White House Garden Is Not Exactly Shovel-Ready." *New York Times*. New York Times Company, 20 Mar. 2009. Web. 12 June 2017.

2. Ibid.

3. Lauren Daniels. "Michelle Obama Bests Ellen DeGeneres in Push-Up Contest." *TIME*. Time, 2 Feb. 2012. Web. 12 June 2017.

4. Ibid.

5. "Remarks by the President and First Lady at the Signing of the Healthy, Hunger-Free Kids Act." *The White House*. The White House, 13 Dec. 2010. Web. 12 June 2017.

6. "Sesame Street: Michelle Obama & the Most Important Meal." *YouTube*. YouTube, 27 July 2014. Web. 12 June 2017.

7. Ibid.

8. Sandra Sobieraj Westfall. "Michelle Obama Throws a Girl Scouts Slumber Party on the White House Lawn." *People*. Time, 30 June 2015. Web. 12 June 2017.

9. Ibid.

10. Tierney McAfee. "First Lady, Sasha and Malia–'Special Girl-Power Unit of Obama Household'– Visit Liberia to Push for Girls' Education." *People*. Time, 23 Sept. 2016. Web. 12 June 2017.

11. "Remarks by the First Lady at City College New York Commencement." *The White House*. The White House, 3 June 2016. Web. 12 June 2017.

12. Ibid.

13. Ibid.

14. "Transcript: Read Michelle Obama's Full Speech from the 2016 DNC." *Washington Post*. Washington Post, 36 July 2016. Web. 12 June 2017.

TO LEARN MORE

Books

Gourley, Robbin. *First Garden: The White House Garden and How It Grew*. New York, NY: Clarion Books, 2011.

Krull, Kathleen. *A Kid's Guide to America's First Ladies*. New York, NY: HarperCollins, 2017.

Stine, Megan. *Who Is Michelle Obama?* New York, NY: Grosset & Dunlap, 2013.

Web Sites

Visit our Web site for links about Michelle Obama: childsworld.com/links

Note to Parents, Teachers, and Librarians: We routinely verify our Web links to make sure they are safe and active sites. So encourage your readers to check them out!

INDEX